W9-AGC-107

Story of
World War II

Peter F. Copeland

DOVER PUBLICATIONS, INC.
Mineola, New York

Introduction

In human terms, World War II remains the most costly war of all time. As many as fifty million people died in the conflict, most of them young. Like World War I, the Second World War was largely fought over conflicting ideologies. In both wars, aristocracy, democracy, fascism, communism, and imperialism played contending parts. From 1939 to 1942, fascism seemed to be the winning ideology: Germany had conquered most of western and southern Europe, and was driving deep into eastern Europe, almost to the borders of Asia. Nazi armies stood at the gates of Alexandria and Cairo in North Africa. Japan had won an immense Pacific empire, and her armies stood poised near the borders of India and Australia.

Two years later, all this had drastically changed.

The heroic resistance of the Soviet Union defeated the German invasion of 1941, and ultimately destroyed the German eastern armies. The western Allies drove the Germans from North Africa and western Europe, and Allied troops were poised for an invasion of the Japanese home islands. Victorious Soviet troops were advancing on the borders of Germany itself.

A year later, in 1945, the Soviets were in Berlin, and the use of atomic weapons had forced Japan to surrender. (Warfare has always spurred advances in technology, and World War II had its share of these, some beneficial, some devastating.)

While the cost of the war in lives and treasure on all sides was enormous, the battles were fought for a cause that was well understood on the Allied side—the defeat of fascism and the preservation of democracy. Although initially reluctant to get involved, the United States entered the war as a result of a direct attack on American forces at Pearl Harbor. Had it not been for the participation of the U.S., the final outcome would undoubtedly have been different.

In any case, the mass of the people in the Allied camp saw the war as a black-and-white battle between good and evil. They acted on a moral imperative whose clarity has not been as apparent in many subsequent conflicts.

Copyright

Copyright © 2004 by Peter F. Copeland
All rights reserved.

Bibliographical Note

Story of World War II is a new work, first published by Dover Publications, Inc., in 2004.

DOVER *Pictorial Archive* SERIES

This book belongs to the Dover Pictorial Archive Series. You may use the designs and illustrations for graphics and crafts applications, free and without special permission, provided that you include no more than four in the same publication or project. (For permission for additional use, please write to Permissions Department, Dover Publications, Inc., 31 East 2nd Street, Mineola, N.Y. 11501.)

However, republication or reproduction of any illustration by any other graphic service, whether it be in a book or in any other design resource, is strictly prohibited.

International Standard Book Number: 0-486-43695-0

Manufactured in the United States of America
Dover Publications, Inc., 31 East 2nd Street, Mineola, N.Y. 11501

1. Polish Lancers Confront German Tanks, September 1939

In September 1939 Germany declared war and attacked Poland over a border dispute. Modern, mechanized units of the German army launched a "blitzkrieg" or "lightning war," racing across the Polish plains toward the capital of Warsaw. The Polish army, despite its brave resistance, could do little to check the swift advance of the German armored columns. Here we see mounted Polish lancers confronting the German tanks. By the end of September the Germans entered the shattered city of Warsaw, and on October 5, the German armed forces staged a victory parade in the streets. The campaign ended with Poland ceasing to exist as a nation, her land divided between Germany and Soviet Russia.

2. A French Border Guard on the Maginot Line, 1939

Although France and England declared war on Germany at the beginning of September 1939 they did little to assist Poland in resisting invasion. The eastern border of France was defended by the seemingly impregnable Maginot Line, a string of fortifications nine miles in depth. Relying on this defensive barrier, the French and their British allies sat quietly while the Germans conquered Poland. The illustration shows a French sentry with his automatic rifle on duty along the Line.

3. The Evacuation of the British Army from Dunkirk, June 1940

In April of 1940 the Germans invaded Norway and Denmark, and though British and French troops went to the assistance of the Norwegians, by May 3, the Germans had forced an Allied evacuation and completed their conquest of Norway. Then on May 10, Germany suddenly invaded and overran Holland and Belgium, and entered northern France, easily bypassing the Maginot Line. In another lightning campaign the Germans split the British and French armies, and forced the evacuation of the British army from Dunkirk, near the French-Belgian border. The evacuation was carried out by a hastily assembled fleet of small boats that ferried the men across the English Channel to safety. Here we see the men of the British rear guard, who defended the beaches of Dunkirk while their army successfully escaped from Europe and returned to England.

4. The Fall of France, June 1940

Paris fell to the Germans on June 14, and the collapse of France followed. On June 19 French military representatives requested an armistice from the German invaders, as shown here. Those British troops still remaining in France, who had escaped capture, were evacuated from Cherbourg and other ports, and landed in western England. On June 21 an armistice ended the fighting, and France became, to all intents and purposes, a German satellite, as did Holland, Belgium, and Luxembourg.

5. The Battle of Britain

In 1940 Britain stood alone against Germany as the German air force (Luftwaffe) began an air offensive over Britain from bases in France. The aim was to destroy the Royal Air Force (RAF) and bomb the island into submission, preparatory to launching an invasion by sea across the English Channel. The Battle of Britain was mainly an air war that lasted into 1941, when German attention was diverted to other fields. There was no invasion of Great Britain, due to the phenomenal success of the RAF in defeating the German air force in the skies over Britain and France. Here we see a German Dornier bomber in flames after having been shot down by an RAF Spitfire fighter over London.

6. War in the African Desert, 1940–41

The Italian dictator Benito Mussolini dragged his country into war by treacherously attacking France from the rear while that nation was struggling to contain the Germans in the spring of 1940. Badly led, and lacking any incentive to fight as an ally of Germany, the Italian armed forces almost immediately suffered an alarming series of setbacks and defeats. In November 1940 the British fleet defeated the main part of the Italian fleet at the port of Taranto in Italy, and in December a series of British victories over Italian colonial forces in North Africa resulted in the capture of Sidi Barrani, an Italian-held village in Egypt. Three Italian generals were taken prisoner, along with 30,000 troops, and tons of supplies, weapons, ammunition, and vehicles. The British entered the Italian North African colony of Libya in pursuit of fleeing Italian forces. The illustration depicts a group of Italian prisoners being conducted to a prison stockade in the western desert.

7. German Invasion of the Balkans, 1941

In the fall of 1940 Mussolini foolishly attacked neighboring Greece from Italian bases in occupied Albania. Within days Greek troops hurled back the Italian advance and invaded Albania in pursuit of the fleeing Italians. Britain sent assistance to the Greeks, and the German dictator Adolf Hitler was forced to come to the aid of his floun-

dering ally, Italy, which he did by launching a surprise attack on Greece and Yugoslavia in April 1941. The Yugoslavian army capitulated on April 17, and Greece was forced to surrender to the invading Germans on April 22. Here we see German bombers flying over Athens and the Acropolis, symbols of the glories of classical Greece.

8. Sinking of the German Battleship *Bismarck,* May 1941

The naval war favored Britain, whose fleet was the largest in the world. Germany sent out large numbers of armed vessels, which were to team up with U-boats in targeting commercial shipping, but were to avoid battle with British warships. In 1939 British cruisers hunted down and destroyed the German pocket battleship *Graf Spee* off the east coast of South America. Two years later, the mighty German battleship *Bismarck,* accompanied by the heavy cruiser, *Prinz Eugen,* evaded the British naval blockade of northern Europe and sailed into the north Atlantic to destroy Allied convoys. The British fleet pursued the German ships and, in a running battle, the *Bismarck* destroyed the British battleship *Hood.* Fighting without air cover, the *Bismarck* was later struck by British torpedo planes and crippled. Surrounded by a British squadron, the German ship was pounded into a flaming wreck, as we see here, until her commander ordered her scuttled. The *Bismarck* went down, carrying most of her crew with her.

9. Operation Barbarossa, the German Invasion of the Soviet Union, June 1941

On June 22, the military might of Nazi Germany was suddenly hurled against Soviet Russia, her former ally. The German attack was launched along a gigantic front, extending from the Baltic to the Black Sea, and was initially remarkably successful. German invaders, advancing in blitzkrieg fashion, surrounded and destroyed a series of Soviet armies, taking millions of prisoners. Russian resistance was fierce, but disorganized by the German tactics, enabling German armored columns to advance toward Moscow and the Ukraine during the spring and summer of 1941. Meanwhile, German armies in the north, with their Finnish allies, surrounded Leningrad. Shown here is a German armored force advancing through a Russian village in flames.

10. Surprise Japanese Attack on Pearl Harbor, Hawaii; December 7, 1941

Japan, Germany's Axis ally in the Pacific, dreamed of building an empire by ousting the British and Dutch from their colonial possessions in Southeast Asia. In order to accomplish this, however, the Japanese had first to cripple or destroy the United States Pacific fleet, the major obstacle to these ambitions. On December 7, 1941, after months of planning and preparation, the Japanese launched a highly successful surprise air attack on the U.S. fleet at Pearl Harbor in Hawaii. Japanese carrier-based torpedo planes and dive-bombers destroyed or seriously damaged six battleships, while other Japanese aircraft attacked and destroyed U.S. Army air forces on the ground, together with hangars and installations. In this illustration Japanese dive-bombers are attacking the battleship U.S.S. *Arizona* at her anchorage at Ford Island. As a result of the attack, the U.S. declared war on Japan on December 8, and on December 10, Germany declared war on the United States.

11. Japanese Conquest of Southeast Asia, 1942

With the U.S. fleet temporarily out of commission, the Japanese army and navy unleashed a multi-pronged offensive on the Asian mainland. The Indo-Chinese colonies of France, the British colonies of Hong Kong, Singapore and the Malay peninsula, and the Dutch East Indies all fell to Japanese forces. In the Philippines the Japanese defeated General Douglas MacArthur and a mixed U.S. and Philippine garrison of the islands. In January 1942 Japanese forces occupied Manila and forced the surrender of surviving U.S. and Filipino forces in May. This illustration shows Japanese infantry officers raising their swords and banners in a Banzai salute celebrating their victory.

12. U.S. Army Carrier-Based Bombers Raid Japan, April 1942

Though the U.S. Pacific fleet was crippled at Pearl Harbor on December 7, the three U.S. aircraft carriers of the Pacific fleet—the *Hornet, Yorktown* and *Lexington*—were at sea at the time, and avoided destruction or damage. The U.S.S. *Hornet,* in April 1942, carried a squadron of U. S. Army Air Force B25 bombers, commanded by General Jimmy Dolittle, that launched a surprise attack on the Japanese home islands. Tokyo, Nagoya, and Yokohama were bombed, and though little real damage was inflicted, the daring raid did a great deal to raise morale in the U.S. The Japanese high command was shocked and humiliated, and was forced to revise their offensive strategy for control of the Pacific.

13. General Erwin Rommel and the Afrika Korps, 1942–43

Half a world away, the German high command decided again to come to the aid of their beleaguered Italian ally in the western deserts of North Africa. The German Afrika Korps, a desert fighting army, was sent to Libya in 1941 under the command of General (later, Field Marshal) Erwin Rommel, one of Germany's leading exponents of "lightning war." Rommel was a spectacular combat leader and strategist, and perhaps the best general Germany produced in World War II. He immediately turned the Italian retreat into a series of impressive victories over the British desert army, earning himself the nickname, "Desert Fox."

14. Malta Holds Out, 1942–43

The small Mediterranean island of Malta, a British possession, was one of the most heavily bombed targets of the entire war. A keystone of the British defense in North Africa, the island was a major impediment to the Axis campaign in the western desert, for it served as a base from which the Allies launched attacks on German and Italian convoys supplying Axis armies in Africa. Thus Malta became a prime target for German and Italian bombers, which rained bombs down on Malta's airfields and naval installations. So intense were the assaults that the Maltese capital city of Valletta (seen here under attack), was bombed an average of eight times a day during the first half of 1942. British convoys carrying food and supplies to Malta were also attacked, and though food and ammunition grew desperately scarce, the island held out and was never invaded by the enemy.

15. The Battle of the Atlantic, 1940–45

In order to bring England to her knees, Admiral Karl Dönitz, head of the German submarine fleet, attempted to starve the country of food and supplies by destroying the fleets of merchant ships that supplied the British Isles. If Britain's lifeline was cut, she would be forced to surrender or starve. Between 1940 and 1943, German U-boats sank thousands of Allied and neutral merchant vessels in the attempt to force England into submission.

The development of the armed convoy system, however, in which merchant ships sailed in convoys with the protection of naval escorts and fleets of accompanying aircraft, eventually cut down Allied losses. Here we see survivors of the crew of a torpedoed Allied freighter escaping in a lifeboat. The fire on the surface of the sea is burning fuel from the ruptured bunker tanks of the sinking freighter.

16. The Soviets Strike Back, Winter 1941–42

The German advance on Moscow stalled in the bitter cold and ice of the Russian winter. Fierce fighting occurred on the central front, but as the Soviets flung fresh Siberian armies into battle, the German advance ground to a halt, and began to crumble away. Hitler refused to allow a German retreat, and took personal command of the army. The German winter defense line held, but at a terrible price—over a million men dead or dying. Here we see white-clad Soviet attackers, armed with submachine guns, advancing over snowy fields with the air support of U.S.-manufactured attack planes.

We Can Do It!

17. Women in the War Effort, U.S.A., 1942–45

The wartime emergency drafted millions of men into the armed forces, opening up a wide range of employment opportunities for women, both in defense industries and the military. In shipyards and factories devoted to the war effort, women built Liberty ships, bombers, and tanks, as well as manufacturing munitions and other war supplies. Others ran streetcars and buses, piloted airplanes and did men's jobs on the farm and in offices. The spirit of patriotic, can-do womanhood was symbolized by posters like this one, featuring a muscular, determined-looking "Rosie the Riveter" dressed in characteristic work shirt and bandana.

18. The Bataan Death March, May 1942

The Japanese conquest of the Philippine islands pro-
ceeded swiftly and successfully. After the Japanese occupation of Manila, a mixed force of 76,000 American and
Philippine defenders, trapped on the Bataan peninsula,
was forced to surrender. The Japanese formed them into
columns and drove them on a forced march of sixty-five
miles to a prison camp. The prisoners were half-starved,
exhausted, and in no condition to endure what became
known as the "Bataan Death March." The Japanese
guards executed those who fell behind or were unable to
continue the grueling march under a blazing sun. Over
ten thousand prisoners died before it was over. Here we
see a scene along the line of the march, drawn from a
photograph taken by a Japanese cameraman.

19. The Battle of Midway, June 1942

The Japanese High Command was obsessed with the idea of a single decisive naval engagement that would eliminate the U.S. fleet once and for all. A previous battle in the Coral Sea had been indecisive, so Japanese admirals decided to seek a fight at Midway Island. One of the most powerful naval forces in Japanese history was assembled to attack Midway, but U.S. cryptanalysts (code breakers) in Hawaii intercepted many of the messages transmitted to the Japanese fleet, and knew that Midway was the objective. The Battle of Midway began on June 4 and lasted four days. Both sides relied heavily on air power. Finally, U.S. dive-bombers attacked the Japanese carriers and in five minutes changed the course of the war in the Pacific. Four Japanese carriers and one heavy cruiser were sunk, while over 330 Japanese planes were lost. The amount of damage fatally crippled the Japanese fleet, which was never the same again. This scene shows U.S. Navy dive-bombers destroying the carrier *Soryu* and a heavy cruiser.

20. The Battle of Stalingrad, August 1942–January 1943

The German plan of battle for the 1942 summer offensive in Soviet Russia called for capturing Leningrad in the north, and Stalingrad in the south, in order to gain access to the rich oil fields of the Caucasus region. German allies—Hungary, Italy, and Romania, among others—supplied fresh armies to make up German losses. In early June, a blitzkrieg attack began with Stalingrad as its goal. By August, the German Sixth Army had reached the Volga River and Stalingrad itself. Here the Soviets put up a desperate, house-to-house, street-by-street fight to save the city that bore the name of Soviet dictator Joseph Stalin. After months of fighting, the Soviets launched a massive counterattack in November, which cut off and surrounded the Sixth Army. Once again, Hitler refused to allow a retreat, and the isolated German force fought on in the ruins of the city. Winter found the blockaded German army beginning to starve, while the wounded died for lack of care and medicine. Finally in January 1943 91,000 survivors of the German Sixth Army surrendered. This illustration depicts a German S.S. trooper surrendering near the body of a comrade.

21. Allied Victory in the Western Desert, November 1942

In the fall of 1942, General (now, Field Marshal) Erwin Rommel was preparing his German Afrika Korps to capture Alexandria and Cairo in Egypt, and to march on the Suez Canal. General Bernard Montgomery commanded the British Eighth Army in the desert. The decisive battle of the North African campaign occurred at the village of El Alamein in Egypt. After stopping Rommel's attack, Montgomery went on the offensive, breaking through the German line and sending the Afrika Korps into a massive retreat. During this confused withdrawal, British tanks surrounded and trapped the fleeing Germans, but Rommel managed to escape into Libya, having lost 60,000 men and most of his tanks and guns. Here we see a German prisoner being assisted to an aid station by two soldiers of the Eighth Army, a force that became known as the "Desert Rats."

22. Operation Torch, the North Africa Landing; November 1942

On November 3, Allied convoys began assembling off the coast of northern Africa, preparing to invade Morocco and Algeria, then under the control of the French Vichy government. The French put up only token resistance—many sought to join the invaders—but German reaction was swift. Led by Field Marshal Erwin Rommel, German troops occupied the neighboring colony of Tunisia, and soon attacked inexperienced American troops at Kasserine Pass, forcing a hasty U.S. retreat. After being stopped again at El Guettar by veterans of the Afrika Korps, the U.S. Army in the field underwent a shakeup; many officers were replaced, and gradually, the green American army group became a seasoned force. With Allied forces facing them in the west, and the British Eighth Army pressing from Libya in the east, the Germans were surrounded. This illustration shows U.S. soldiers coming ashore under the cover of U.S. Army Air Force fighter planes.

23. The Casablanca Conference, January 1943

In January of 1943, President Franklin Delano Roosevelt and British Prime Minister Winston Churchill met at Casablanca in North Africa. They announced the Allied policy that there would be no negotiations with Germany—the Allies demanded unconditional surrender. This was done to appease Soviet dictator Joseph Stalin, whose Red Army was attempting to turn back the German invasion of his country and destroy the German army. Critics of this policy said that this declaration only made the Germans fight that much harder. Churchill and Roosevelt, however, were in total agreement on this policy, which was, in fact, carried out.

24. Defeat of the German Afrika Korps, May 1943

Surrounded by enemies and cut off from supplies and ammunition, the Afrika Korps fought on in the Tunisian desert. However, their tanks had been destroyed or were out of fuel, and their food was almost gone. With the fall of the capital of Tunis, German General von Arnim surrendered 275,000 German and Italian troops on May 12, 1943. Depicted here is a German soldier, shot amid the wreckage of the Afrika Korps in the Tunisian desert. Though the Korps ceased to exist from this point on, Field Marshal Rommel escaped to Europe before the surrender.

25. Battle of Kursk, July 1943

Following the disastrous German defeat at Stalingrad, Adolf Hitler, now commanding the German army, gathered his armored divisions for a final battle to annihilate the Red Army armored forces. At Kursk, in the Ukraine, a half million German troops, in seventeen armored divisions, attacked a Soviet army awaiting them. An overwhelming series of artillery barrages stopped the German attack, after which the Soviets immediately advanced in what was to become their first summer offensive of the war. The German front shattered and crumbled, allowing the Red Army to retake the Ukrainian cities of Orel, Kharkov, Smolensk, and Kiev, before the end of autumn. This scene shows wrecked German tanks amid fields of summer sunflowers at the end of the Battle of Kursk.

26. German U-boat Defeat at Sea, 1943–44

In the first seven months of 1942, German U-boats sank 681 Allied ships. However, as U.S. radar gradually improved, and navy and air force planes began patrolling the sea-lanes, Allied losses diminished. Moreover, when long-range Allied aircraft operating from Iceland, Canada, and Northern Ireland began hunting down and destroying the undersea raiders, U-boat losses increased dramatically. By mid-1943 almost three quarters of the original U-boat force had been destroyed. Here we see a U.S. Army bomber attacking a U-boat on the surface, while an Allied convoy sails by on the horizon.

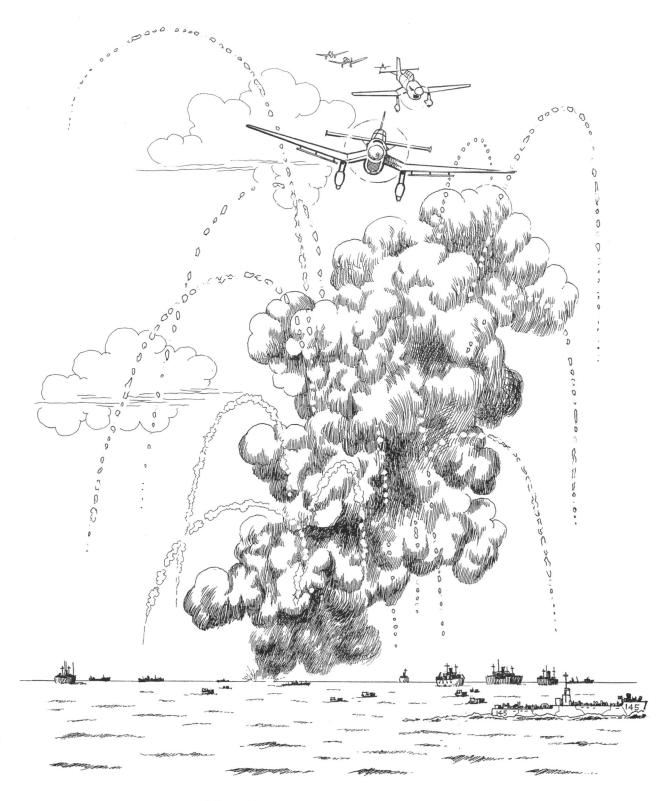

27. Allied Invasion of Sicily, July 1943

The commitment of massive armed forces in North Africa made an Allied invasion of southern Europe almost inevitable. The invasion and occupation of Sicily would deprive the Axis powers of air bases on that island, and would pave the way for the invasion of the rest of Italy, giving the Allies a toehold on the European continent. British and American troops landed unexpectedly in Sicily on July 9, amid high seas and gale-force winds. The Germans opposed the invaders, but most Italians offered only token resistance and quickly surrendered. Indeed, the Sicilians welcomed the Allies with flowers and wine. German defense of the island was determined and stubborn, but ultimately some 60,000 German troops escaped across the Straits of Messina to fight another day in Italy.

28. The Fall of Benito Mussolini, July 1943

By mid-1943 the Italian people were heartily sick of the war, the German alliance, and dictator Benito Mussolini. Italy was about to become a battleground, and King Victor Emmanuel, together with members of the Italian government, decided that Mussolini had to go, and that Italy must change sides or leave the war. Dismissed and replaced by the King, Mussolini was taken as a prisoner to a mountain resort in Abruzzi. There airborne German S.S. men, on Hitler's orders, rescued (or perhaps kidnapped) him from the ski lodge in which he was being held. Mussolini was brought to Hitler's headquarters and forced to become the puppet dictator of a Fascist republic under German control. Two years later, the broken leader of Fascism in Italy was captured by Communist partisan fighters and brutally executed. Mussolini is shown here, in civilian clothes, escorted by his German captors/rescuers to a meeting with Hitler in September of 1943.

29. Allied Invasion of Italy, September 1943

The Allied invasion of the Italian mainland occurred during negotiations between the Italian government and the Allied High Command, which brought Italy over to the Allied side. Alarmed, the Germans flooded Italy with troops, disarmed the Italian Army and began turning the Italian peninsula into a fortress. British troops landed in Calabria in southern Italy without too much trouble, but U.S. troops landing at Salerno faced stiff opposition that nearly drove them back into the sea. Allied naval and air forces provided such devastating supporting fire, however, that the Germans were forced to withdraw. The U.S. Army then began a northward drive with 135,000 men and 30,000 vehicles. Italy had now become a major battleground; the Germans fought a rearguard action as they withdrew north, making the Allies pay a heavy price for every foot of mountainous terrain. This illustration shows U.S. troops going ashore at Salerno, while naval gunners fight off the attack of German dive-bombers.

30. German Retreat in Soviet Russia, September 1943

On September 26 Radio Berlin announced the heaviest German defeat of 1943. The Russian city of Smolensk had been recaptured by the Soviets and the Red Army was advancing on all fronts. By October, Soviet troops were moving twelve to fifteen miles a day, and the once-mighty German army was fleeing before them. In the south the Red Army closed a trap on 90,000 Germans retreating in the Crimea. Meanwhile, Marshall Tito, Communist commander of Yugoslavian partisan fighters, was conducting a successful guerilla war, tying up thousands of German occupiers in that country. Depicted here are German soldiers, carrying their wounded in disorganized retreat before the advancing Red Army.

31. The Teheran Conference, November 1943

In November of 1943, the leaders of the Allied powers—Roosevelt, Churchill, and Stalin—met in Teheran, capital of Iran. For two years, the Soviets had been struggling with the heavy burden of the war against Hitler, and Stalin was press-ing his allies to open a second front in western Europe, a landing in France, that would draw off German troops from the Russian front. At Teheran, the decision was made and acted upon: an invasion of France would take place within a year.

32. The Allied Drive to Liberate Rome, June 1944

Rome was the first Axis capital to be liberated. On June 4, 1944, crowds of jubilant Italians greeted American troops as the Allied Fifth Army entered the city. Fortunately, the travails of war had not impaired the glory and grandeur of the Eternal City, or destroyed her ancient monuments and temples. This picture shows citizens of Rome happily greeting their liberators.

33. The Holocaust, 1940–45

As Allied troops penetrated Hitler's Europe from east and west, they discovered horrifying evidence of the inhuman treatment meted out to those whom Hitler had judged to be unworthy of survival. Between 1939 and 1945 millions of innocent people were tortured and murdered in concentration camps in a campaign of genoci-dal destruction unmatched in the history of the world. The vast majority were Jews, but gypsies, the mentally ill and others were also systematically executed by the Nazis in pursuit of their plan for a new, racially pure society. Shown here are two victims of the camps, behind barbed wire, as seen by their American liberators.

34. D-day, the Allied Invasion of France; June 1944

Early on the morning of June 6, 1944, thousands of American, Canadian, and British soldiers, under cover of the greatest air and sea bombardment in history, landed on the coast of Normandy. Airborne forces had been dropped the previous night and were already dug in behind the German lines. The defenders were stunned by the ferocity of the Allied artillery barrage, but still managed to put up stiff resistance as Allied soldiers came ashore. Many never made it past the beaches. Here we see U.S. troops landing at Omaha Beach on the morning of June 6.

35. The Plot to Kill Hitler, July 1944

By mid-1944 it was becoming apparent that Germany was losing the war. Seeking to eliminate or replace Hitler, a group of high-ranking officers on the general staff (including Field Marshal Rommel) hatched a plot to set off a bomb in Hitler's military headquarters during a staff conference. Hitler was not killed or even injured by the blast, but for some hours confusion reigned as some German officers even arrested each other. By the following morning Hitler himself announced that he was in control, and that the plotters were being rounded up or had already been executed. For months afterward, in fact until the end of the war, a wholesale purge of the general staff continued. Many officers and highly placed civilians were executed after a series of hastily conducted show trials. This picture shows Hitler and some of his generals at a strategy conference.

36. The Soviet Assault in the East, 1944–45

The general Soviet offensive that began in July 1944 resulted in a rout of the German armies in the east. The whole German line gave way, from the Baltic in the north to the Carpathian Mountains in the south. Russian forces pursued the fleeing Germans through the Ukraine and Poland, and were soon approaching East Prussia in Germany, where the Germans were desperately trying to form a defensive line. Estonia and Latvia on the Baltic Sea were overrun, and on August 5, the Soviets crossed the border into Germany. Depicted here is a dazed German soldier next to his disabled 88mm gun, as Red Army soldiers and tanks advance in the background.

37. The Allied Breakout from Normandy, July 1944

In July the Allies broke through the German defense line on the Cherbourg peninsula, and armored columns began racing toward Paris as German opposition collapsed. On August 15, a massive armada of ships landed another invading Allied army on the shores of southern France under cover of heavy naval and air bombardment.

Again, as in the Normandy landing, airborne troops parachuted behind enemy lines. Here we see a U.S. armored column that has stopped to consult maps and take a break, before resuming their advance toward the French capital.

38. Underground Resistance to German Occupation in Europe, 1942–45

Resistance groups in occupied countries now began active operations more openly than before, harassing retreating Germans, and blowing up transportation systems and German supply dumps. As we see here, they also dealt harshly with collaborationists and German agents among their own people, whom they regarded as traitors. Some underground fighters were Communists who often had their own political agenda, while others were simply patriots who hated the German occupiers of their country. Here fighters have cornered a suspected collaborator beneath a pro-Allies "V for Victory" sign painted on a fence.

39. Allied Liberation of Paris, August 1944

On August 23, French Radio in London made a premature announcement that after four years of tyranny, Paris had been liberated. In fact, it was not until two days later that the city was no longer under German domination. The vanguard of the liberating Allied forces was a column of General LeClerc's Free French troops that reached the heart of Paris amid the wild acclaim of the Parisians. On August 25 French headquarters announced that the German commander of Paris had surrendered to General LeClerc. Fortunately, since Paris had not been fought over or heavily bombed, the liberators found the city much the same as it had been when they had last seen it in 1940. In this scene General Charles de Gaulle, commander of the Free French forces, walks the streets of Paris with an enthusiastic crowd of admirers.

40. Liberation of the Philippines, October 1944–June 1945

The Philippines had chafed under the iron rule of Japan. Guerrilla fighters took to the bush to resist, and the people waited impatiently for the return of the Americans. The Japanese had promised the islands their independence and participation in a Conference of the Nations of Greater East Asia, but in fact they proved to be cruel, hard conquerors, and most Filipinos hated them. Liberation began in October 1944 with U.S. landings on Leyte, where American troops were joyfully greeted by Filipino guerrilla fighters and civilians. When U.S. forces landed on Luzon and began the battle to liberate Manila, Filipinos happily assisted them despite savage Japanese vengeance wreaked upon the population of the city. During house-to-house fighting, Japanese soldiers murdered Filipino citizens by the thousands, and reduced the once-beautiful city to a ruin strewn with corpses. This illustration shows General MacArthur coming ashore on Luzon, fulfilling the pledge he made in 1942: "I shall return."

41. The Battle of the Bulge, December 1944–January 1945

As Germany was attempting to repulse American attacks against the Siegfried Line (a series of fortifications and tank defenses facing the Maginot Line) on the western border of Germany, Adolf Hitler was at the same time planning a surprise attack on the Allied forces. This was to take place in the forest of the Ardennes, where, in 1940, he had broken through the British and French armies. His objective was to capture Antwerp and hopefully, create another Dunkirk for the Allies. No one in the Allied camp had even dreamed of the possibility of a German attack, since Germany was fighting a losing defensive battle on all fronts. The German assault in winter was a complete surprise, and at first achieved an amazing success. As it turned out, however, the Germans did not have the men or the tanks to overcome the strong Allied forces, and eventually, the offensive was slowed and then thrown back. Here we see American troops encircled and pinned down in the town of Bastogne in Belgium, trying to hold off the German attack.

42. The Fall of Berlin, April–May 1945

On April 12, 1945, President Franklin Roosevelt died and Harry Truman became the thirty-third president of the United States. Roosevelt did not live to see Berlin fall, after a titanic battle, to the Red Army. The fight for the city had been desperate, but ultimately hopeless for its defenders. Here Nazism made its last stand against its sworn Communist enemy, inflicting an estimated 300,000 casualties on the Red Army. As the Russians closed in, Hitler died by his own hand in his underground bunker beneath the ruined city. On May 7, 1945, the German armed forces surrendered unconditionally at Rheims in France; the surrender was repeated the next day at Soviet headquarters in Berlin. May 8 became known in the West as VE day (Victory in Europe day). The illustration depicts a Soviet soldier raising the Red flag on the roof of the German Reichstag in Berlin, on April 20, 1945.

43. The Battles of Iwo Jima and Okinawa, February–June 1945

The bloody battles of Iwo Jima and Okinawa marked the last campaigns of the Pacific war. The eight square miles of Iwo Jima were defended by more than 20,000 Japanese, who were prepared for the Allied attack. The marines who took the island had to fight every inch of the way, taking almost 21,000 casualties in the 26-day battle, which prompted General Holland M. Smith to say that it was the toughest fight for the U.S. Marine Corps in its 168-year history. Okinawa, only 350 miles from the Japanese home islands, was defended by 100,000 men and a squadron of suicide planes, which severely damaged the U.S. fleet. As at Iwo Jima, soldiers and marines had to dig out the fanatic defenders one-by-one in a long, bloody battle that did not end until almost 50,000 U.S. casualties had been counted. Shown here are marines raising the flag over Mount Suribachi on Iwo Jima, in a drawing done from the famous photograph taken by Joe Rosenthal.

44. Dropping the First Atomic Bomb; August 6, 1945

At 8:15 A.M. on August 6, 1945, the crew of the American B29 bomber *Enola Gay* dropped the first atomic bomb over the Japanese city of Hiroshima. On August 9, another bomb was dropped on the city of Nagasaki. The destruction in each case was staggering. Between seventy and eighty thousand people died at Hiroshima, and some forty thousand lost their lives at Nagasaki. This unprecedented attack had the desired effect: the Japanese Emperor Hirohito ordered his government to present Japan's surrender to the Allies. On August 10, Tokyo agreed to the terms the Allies demanded, namely, unconditional surrender. Five days later, the Emperor broadcast to the Japanese people that the war was over, and that Japan had accepted the Allied terms. This illustration depicts the *Enola Gay,* having dropped the first atomic bomb, unleashing the specter of atomic weapons which still haunts the world.

45. Japanese Surrender; September 2, 1945

There were several Japanese "surrenders" on widely separated fronts—in China, the East Indies, and other parts of the former Japanese Empire—as well as small unit and individual surrenders at many places. The principal surrender, however, took place aboard the U.S. Navy battleship *Missouri* in Tokyo Bay, on September 2, 1945. The Japanese foreign minister and the chief of the Japanese general staff signed for the Japanese Empire, as shown here. Lieutenant General Jonathan Wainwright, who had surrendered U.S. forces on Bataan in 1943, and Lieutenant General Sir Arthur Percival, the man who "lost" Singapore, signed for the Allies, followed by General Douglas MacArthur, Admiral Chester Nimitz, and other Allied delegates. General MacArthur then announced "these proceedings are closed," and World War II was over.